AI Odyssey: From the Dot-Com Boom to the Age of Intelligence

Table of Contents

www.ingramcontent.com/pod-product-compliance
Lightning Source LLC
LaVergne TN
LVHW022126060326
832903LV00063B/4119

Introduction: A New Frontier of Innovation

In the late 1990s, a wave of innovation swept across the globe. The Dot-Com Era emerged as a time of wild ambition, rapid experimentation, and transformative ideas that redefined communication, commerce, and culture. During those heady years, startup founders, venture capitalists, and technologists chased the promise of a new digital world, often disregarding conventional wisdom in favor of bold, untested ideas. Today, as we stand at the threshold of a revolution powered by artificial intelligence (AI), we find ourselves looking back at that seminal period—not with nostalgia alone, but with a sense of continuity. The same entrepreneurial spirit that fueled the internet boom now permeates the laboratories, boardrooms, and coding dens of the AI revolution.

This book, *AI Odyssey: From the Dot-Com Boom to the Age of Intelligence.* It examines how the legacy of the Dot-Com boom—characterized by rapid innovation, risk-taking, and a relentless pursuit of the next big thing—has laid the groundwork for the current transformation in artificial intelligence. As digital technologies continue to evolve at a breakneck pace, we are witnessing a convergence of historical momentum and cutting-edge breakthroughs, promising to reshape the very fabric of our society.

The Dot-Com Era was defined by an explosive growth of internet companies, fueled by the advent of new digital infrastructures and the democratization of information. Studies have shown that during this period, venture capital investments increased exponentially, driving unprecedented levels of technological experimentation and disruption. For example, research by the McKinsey Global Institute documented how digital startups not only altered traditional business models but also reconfigured consumer expectations around immediacy and connectivity. Although many companies succumbed to the harsh realities of market correction, the era's spirit of innovation left an indelible mark on the tech landscape.

Today, artificial intelligence is charting a similar course. According to a recent report from Deloitte, 61% of executives have accelerated their AI initiatives in response to the digital transformation imperatives accelerated by the COVID-19 pandemic. AI is no longer a niche field confined to academic labs or science fiction fantasies—it is a driving force behind innovations in healthcare, finance, transportation, and beyond. In many ways, the AI revolution is poised to be even more transformative than the internet boom, as it promises not only to enhance existing technologies but to redefine what machines can do.

Yet, as with the Dot-Com bubble, the promise of AI comes with its own set of challenges and risks. The Dot-Com Era taught us valuable lessons about speculative excess, market volatility, and the perils of unbridled optimism. While the internet ultimately matured into a robust platform for global commerce and communication, its early days were marred by dramatic highs and precipitous lows. In a similar vein, the rise of AI is accompanied by concerns about job displacement, ethical dilemmas, and the potential concentration of power among a few dominant players. Studies by the World Economic Forum suggest that while AI could displace millions of jobs in the next decade, it also has the potential to create new roles that we can scarcely imagine today—if society is prepared to manage the transition responsibly.

This book does not merely catalog the technological achievements of our time. It seeks to understand the underlying ethos of innovation that emerged during the Dot-Com Era and explore how that spirit can be harnessed to address the complex challenges of AI today. We delve into how the same mix of audacity, creativity, and calculated risk-taking that once propelled internet startups can now be applied to developing AI systems that are both revolutionary and ethically sound.

A central theme of our exploration is the concept of exponential growth. The Dot-Com Era was characterized by a seemingly unbounded acceleration of digital innovation—a phenomenon often described by the law of accelerating returns. Pioneers like Ray Kurzweil famously predicted that technological progress would eventually reach a "singularity," a point where the pace of change becomes virtually incomprehensible. Recent studies in innovation economics have reinforced the idea that growth in digital technologies follows a hyperbolic curve, where initial incremental improvements rapidly compound into groundbreaking leaps forward. In the realm of AI, this acceleration is visible in the rapid improvements in machine learning algorithms, natural language processing, and computer vision over the past decade. For instance, a study published in *Nature* highlighted that state-of-the-art language models have improved their performance exponentially in recent years, a trend that is likely to continue.

Another key element is the democratization of technology. During the Dot-Com boom, the internet lowered the barriers to entry for entrepreneurs, enabling a diverse array of innovators to contribute to the digital ecosystem. Today, open-source platforms and cloud computing services are democratizing access to AI development tools. This has led to a vibrant community of researchers and developers who are not only pushing the boundaries of what AI can achieve but also ensuring that its benefits are more broadly shared. Research by the OpenAI organization, for instance, has shown that collaborative approaches to AI development can accelerate progress while also helping to distribute both risks and rewards more equitably.

However, the rapid pace of innovation also brings with it significant risks. The Dot-Com bubble eventually burst because of over-speculation and a lack of sustainable business models. In the context of AI, there is a growing chorus of voices—from academics to industry leaders—warning about the dangers of deploying unregulated systems. The Future of Life Institute has repeatedly emphasized the need for robust ethical frameworks and governance structures to guide AI development, arguing that without proper oversight, AI could exacerbate social inequalities or even lead to unintended catastrophic outcomes.

In addressing these issues, we must consider not only the technical aspects of AI but also the human dimensions. How do we ensure that AI systems are designed with empathy and social responsibility in mind? How can we build institutions that are capable of managing the profound changes that AI promises to bring? These questions resonate with the lessons learned from the Dot-Com Era. Just as that period forced society to confront the disruptive impacts of rapid digital transformation, the rise of AI challenges us to rethink the balance between innovation and regulation, between progress and preservation.

One promising avenue lies in interdisciplinary research. Studies in cognitive science, ethics, and computer science are beginning to converge, providing new insights into how AI systems can be designed to align with human values. For example, the field of explainable AI (XAI) seeks to create models that not only perform complex tasks but also offer transparent and interpretable insights into their decision-making processes. This is critical for building trust among users and ensuring that AI technologies can be audited and held accountable. Similarly, research in human-computer interaction (HCI) is exploring ways to design interfaces that promote collaboration and mutual understanding between humans and machines—a crucial step toward realizing an AI revolution that enhances rather than diminishes our humanity.

As we explore these topics in depth, it is important to recognize that the journey from the Dot-Com Era to the AI revolution is not a simple linear progression. It is a complex, dynamic process marked by both leaps forward and occasional setbacks. The entrepreneurial zeal of the Dot-Com days did not guarantee sustained success overnight, and neither will the innovations in AI be free of challenges. Rather, both eras illustrate the iterative nature of technological progress—a continuous cycle of trial, error, adaptation, and reinvention.

The lessons of the past are particularly instructive when we consider the societal implications of AI. The Dot-Com Era was as much about cultural transformation as it was about technological advancement. It reshaped consumer behavior, redefined business models, and even altered our perceptions of community and identity. In many ways, AI is poised to have an even more profound impact on our social fabric. As machines become more integrated into our daily lives—from personalized digital assistants to intelligent systems that influence our access to information—they will inevitably challenge our notions of privacy, autonomy, and even what it means to be human.

In this light, our exploration is not solely about celebrating technological breakthroughs; it is also about grappling with the ethical, social, and economic questions that arise when innovation outpaces our traditional regulatory and cultural frameworks. The rapid advancement of AI, much like the internet before it, compels us to ask: Who benefits from these technologies, and at what cost? How do we ensure that the next wave of innovation does not leave behind the very human values that underpin our society? These are the questions that we will address as we journey together through the chapters of this book.

As we stand at this crossroads, the call to action is clear: We must harness the entrepreneurial spirit and innovative energy of the Dot-Com Era to guide the development of AI in ways that are ethical, inclusive, and forward-thinking. This book aims to serve as both a retrospective of lessons learned and a roadmap for navigating the challenges ahead. It invites readers—from tech enthusiasts and business leaders to policymakers and everyday citizens—to engage with these critical issues and envision a future where technology and humanity thrive in harmony.

In the chapters that follow, we will delve deeper into the historical roots of the Dot-Com spirit, exploring the trials, triumphs, and transformative ideas that defined an era. We will examine how that same spirit is now driving the breakthroughs in AI and what it means for the future of innovation. By understanding where we have come from, we can better navigate the complexities of the present and chart a course toward a future that leverages technology for the greater good.

With this foundation in place, our journey continues into the next chapter, where we will explore the evolution of digital innovation and the enduring lessons of the Dot-Com Era—a story of ambition, resilience, and the relentless pursuit of progress that continues to shape our world today.

Chapter 1: The Dot-Com Era – A Blueprint for Digital Disruption

In the annals of modern technology, few periods have captured the imagination and ambition of innovators quite like the Dot-Com Era. This chapter delves into that seminal period—a time when a brave new digital landscape was just beginning to take shape, when every click held the promise of a revolution, and when a handful of daring entrepreneurs risked it all to redefine the boundaries of possibility. By examining the origins, the explosive growth, and the inevitable lessons learned during this era, we can begin to understand the enduring spirit that now fuels the ongoing AI revolution.

The Dawn of the Digital Age

The mid-to-late 1990s marked a profound transformation in the way information was created, shared, and consumed. With the advent of the World Wide Web, a once-niche network designed primarily for academic and governmental use burst into the mainstream. Suddenly, anyone with a computer and a dial-up connection could access a global repository of knowledge—a concept that, until then, had belonged solely to the realm of science fiction.

During this period, the internet was more than just a tool; it was a catalyst for radical change. Entrepreneurs saw opportunity where others saw uncertainty. For many, the internet represented a blank canvas, an open frontier where traditional rules no longer applied. In this fertile environment, ideas spread with unprecedented speed, and the barriers to entry for launching new businesses were dramatically lowered. As noted in a McKinsey Global Institute study, venture capital investments in internet startups surged during these years, driven by a potent mix of innovation, market excitement, and a willingness to gamble on unproven business models.

A Culture of Experimentation and Risk

What truly defined the Dot-Com Era was its culture—a culture steeped in experimentation, risk-taking, and an almost evangelical belief in the transformative power of technology. Startups sprouted like wildflowers in Silicon Valley and beyond, each fueled by a belief that the next big idea was just around the corner. Office spaces were filled with open-plan workstations, beanbag chairs, and the palpable energy of teams working around the clock to build a digital future.

The era was marked by a relentless pursuit of rapid growth, often at the expense of conventional financial wisdom. Companies were valued not on their current profitability, but on their potential to capture a future market that, to many investors, seemed limitless. This speculative approach led to sky-high valuations and a frenetic pace of innovation, where the primary currency was not cash flow but disruptive ideas. A study by Harvard Business Review later argued that this mindset—though it eventually led to market corrections—was essential in driving the early breakthroughs that would set the stage for the robust digital economy we enjoy today.

The Rise, Fall, and Enduring Legacy

Inevitably, however, the exuberance of the Dot-Com Era led to a dramatic correction. By the early 2000s, it became painfully clear that many companies had overestimated both the speed and sustainability of the digital revolution. The bubble burst in a spectacular fashion, wiping out vast sums of venture capital and leaving a trail of failed enterprises in its wake. Yet, rather than marking the end of the internet's promise, the collapse served as a vital learning experience.

The lessons of the Dot-Com bust were manifold. It highlighted the importance of sustainable business models, the need for disciplined growth strategies, and the risks inherent in chasing unbridled innovation without a solid foundation. While many companies failed, others—such as Amazon, eBay, and

Google—weathered the storm and emerged stronger, having learned to balance visionary thinking with prudent financial management. These survivors went on to build the backbone of the modern digital economy, proving that even in failure there are seeds of enduring success.

Innovation Under Pressure: A Study in Resilience

Research conducted by the Boston Consulting Group and corroborated by studies from Gartner emphasizes that periods of market correction, though painful, often lead to a more resilient and mature ecosystem. The Dot-Com Era's collapse forced entrepreneurs and investors alike to reassess their strategies and adopt a more measured approach to innovation. Companies that survived the downturn did so by focusing on customer needs, investing in technology infrastructure, and building scalable models that could withstand market volatility.

This recalibration of strategy is echoed in today's approach to AI. Just as the internet matured through a series of boom and bust cycles, the field of artificial intelligence is evolving in a similarly iterative manner. Early experiments in AI were marked by rapid progress and equally swift setbacks. Yet, with each cycle, the technology has grown more robust, its applications more refined, and its potential more clearly understood. The resilience born out of the Dot-Com correction provides a valuable blueprint for navigating the uncertainties inherent in the current AI landscape.

The Spirit of the Dot-Com: More Than Just Technology

Beyond the technical innovations, the Dot-Com Era instilled a set of cultural values and an entrepreneurial ethos that continue to resonate today. It was a time when failure was not stigmatized but viewed as an essential part of the learning process—a necessary risk in the pursuit of radical change. This mindset, encapsulated by the mantra "fail fast, learn faster," has become a cornerstone of tech culture, shaping the way startups approach both opportunity and adversity.

In many respects, the same ethos is driving the AI revolution. Modern tech companies are not merely looking to build smarter algorithms; they are striving to create systems that fundamentally alter how we work, communicate, and interact with the world. The willingness to embrace uncertainty, to iterate rapidly, and to learn from mistakes is what sets the best innovators apart from the rest. It is this same spirit of audacity and adaptability that the survivors of the Dot-Com bubble have passed down to the next generation of digital pioneers.

Bridging Past and Present: Lessons for the AI Revolution

The connection between the Dot-Com Era and the present AI revolution is more than a historical curiosity—it is a powerful lens through which we can view today's technological challenges. The early internet was built on a foundation of shared knowledge, open collaboration, and the relentless pursuit of innovation. These principles remain crucial as we confront the ethical, social, and economic dilemmas posed by AI.

For instance, consider the importance of data transparency and accountability. During the Dot-Com Era, the democratization of information transformed how businesses operated and how consumers interacted with the market. Today, as AI systems become increasingly integrated into every facet of our lives, the need for transparency in how these systems function is paramount. Studies published in journals such as *IEEE Transactions on Neural Networks and Learning Systems* have underscored the importance of explainable AI—systems that not only make decisions but also provide insight into the rationale behind those decisions. This drive for clarity and accountability is a direct inheritance from the Dot-Com period, where open-source projects and collaborative platforms laid the groundwork for a more transparent digital future.

Another critical lesson lies in the balance between innovation and regulation. The exuberance of the Dot-Com Era eventually gave way to a more structured, regulated environment as governments and regulatory bodies sought to mitigate the risks associated with unbridled growth. In the realm of AI, similar tensions are emerging. On one hand, rapid innovation is essential to unlock the full potential of AI; on the other hand, without appropriate safeguards, there is a risk that these technologies could exacerbate inequalities or lead to unintended negative consequences. Learning from the past, policymakers and industry leaders today are beginning to craft frameworks that aim to balance these competing imperatives, ensuring that the AI revolution proceeds in a manner that is both dynamic and responsible.

A Catalyst for the Future

The Dot-Com Era was not merely a period of technological innovation—it was a catalyst that fundamentally redefined society's relationship with technology. It altered the way we perceive communication, commerce, and even community. As we move forward into the age of artificial intelligence, the echoes of that era continue to influence our trajectory. The boldness, the failures, and ultimately the successes of the Dot-Com period serve as both a warning and an inspiration. They remind us that technological revolutions are rarely linear; they are complex, often messy, and always full of surprises.

Recent surveys by the Pew Research Center highlight a growing public awareness of the profound changes brought about by digital technologies. While there is both excitement and apprehension about the future, there is also a consensus that the lessons of the past are invaluable. The same study noted that people who lived through the Dot-Com boom—whether as entrepreneurs, employees, or everyday users—tend to view today's digital innovations with a mix of cautious optimism and informed skepticism. This collective memory, passed down through decades of technological evolution, forms a crucial backdrop as we chart the future of AI.

Carrying the Legacy Forward

As we reflect on the transformative power of the Dot-Com Era, it becomes evident that the spirit of innovation, risk-taking, and relentless experimentation is not confined to a single moment in history. Instead, it is an ongoing legacy—a blueprint that continues to guide the evolution of technology. The lessons learned during that time, from both spectacular successes and crushing failures, provide a rich repository of knowledge that modern innovators can draw upon. This legacy is now being reinterpreted in the context of artificial intelligence, as we seek to harness the same transformative energy while avoiding the pitfalls of the past.

In many ways, the Dot-Com Era was the crucible in which today's digital culture was forged. Its influence is seen in everything from the open-source movement to the startup culture that prizes agility and innovation. As we stand on the brink of the AI revolution, these cultural and technological foundations offer both a roadmap and a set of guiding principles. They remind us that while the tools and platforms may change, the core values of curiosity, collaboration, and a willingness to take calculated risks remain as vital as ever.

In tracing the arc of the Dot-Com Era—from its explosive birth and dizzying growth to its eventual collapse and subsequent transformation—we gain a clearer understanding of the forces that have shaped our digital world. The era was a testament to human ingenuity and the relentless pursuit of progress, even in the face of uncertainty and risk. Its lessons, both cautionary and inspirational, serve as the bedrock upon which the AI revolution is being built.

As we turn our focus to the present, the question that naturally arises is: How can we apply these hard-won lessons to the emerging challenges of artificial intelligence? In the chapters that follow, we will explore the evolution of AI itself—from early experiments in machine learning to today's advanced systems capable of understanding and generating human language. We will examine how the same spirit of the Dot-Com Era is fueling innovations that promise to redefine our world, and how the balance between visionary thinking and practical oversight is more crucial now than ever before.

This journey from the past to the future is not a simple retracing of steps; it is an unfolding narrative where each chapter builds on the insights of the previous one. The legacy of the Dot-Com Era is not a closed chapter in history—it is a living, evolving blueprint that continues to influence the direction of technological innovation. As we close this chapter, we invite you to carry forward the lessons of relentless experimentation, risk management, and transformative vision. In our next chapter, we will delve deeper into the evolution of artificial intelligence itself, exploring its origins, its rapid development, and the foundational technologies that are driving its growth. The stage is set, and the journey into the heart of AI awaits.

Chapter 2: The Evolution of Artificial Intelligence – From Inception to the Deep Learning Revolution

In the same way that the early pioneers of the Dot-Com Era transformed a nascent network into a global phenomenon, the field of artificial intelligence has followed its own remarkable evolution—a journey that spans decades of scientific inquiry, serendipitous breakthroughs, and relentless experimentation. In this chapter, we trace the origins of AI, examine the key technological milestones that have propelled its rapid development, and explore the foundational technologies that continue to drive its growth today.

The Seeds of a Dream

The idea of machines that can think and learn is not a product of our modern digital age. Its origins stretch back to the early 20th century and even further into philosophical musings about the nature of mind and intelligence. In the 1940s, the visionary work of mathematicians and logicians, such as Alan Turing, laid the groundwork for what would later become artificial intelligence. Turing's seminal 1950 paper, *Computing Machinery and Intelligence*, introduced the concept of the Turing Test—a simple, yet profound criterion for machine intelligence. He asked, "Can machines think?" and suggested that if a machine's responses were indistinguishable from those of a human, it might be said to possess intelligence.

This question not only spurred scientific curiosity but also captured the public imagination. Turing's ideas, though formulated in a time when computers were the size of rooms, planted the seeds for the dream of a thinking machine—a dream that would, over the next several decades, slowly transform into reality.

The Dawn of Symbolic AI

The 1950s and 1960s witnessed the birth of what is now known as symbolic or "good old-fashioned" AI (GOFAI). Early AI researchers believed that human thought could be replicated through a series of logical rules and symbolic representations. During the Dartmouth Conference in 1956, which is widely regarded as the birth of AI as an academic discipline, scientists set out to create systems that could mimic human reasoning using formal logic. Programs like the Logic Theorist and the General Problem Solver were developed to solve puzzles and prove mathematical theorems. These early systems were ingenious in their design, yet their capabilities were limited by the computational resources available at the time and the inherent complexity of encoding human knowledge in symbolic form.

Despite these limitations, the symbolic approach laid critical groundwork. It taught researchers that the path to machine intelligence was as much about understanding human reasoning as it was about building hardware. However, by the late 1970s, it became clear that purely symbolic systems struggled to deal with the messy, ambiguous nature of real-world data.

The Rise of Expert Systems

In the 1980s, the focus shifted from abstract problem-solving to more practical applications. The concept of expert systems emerged—computer programs that emulated the decision-making abilities of human experts in specific domains, such as medical diagnosis or financial analysis. These systems used extensive rule-based frameworks, often crafted with the help of human experts, to interpret and act on complex information. One notable example was MYCIN, a system developed for identifying bacteria and recommending antibiotics. MYCIN demonstrated that even with limited computational power, carefully engineered AI could provide real value in specialized fields.

While expert systems enjoyed commercial success and widespread adoption in certain industries, they were inherently brittle. Their reliance on handcrafted rules meant that they lacked the flexibility to adapt to new, unforeseen situations—a challenge that would eventually prompt researchers to explore more dynamic approaches.

The Neural Network Renaissance

The limitations of symbolic AI and expert systems led to a gradual but profound shift in focus during the late 1980s and early 1990s—toward neural networks, a computational paradigm inspired by the human brain. Early neural network models, like the perceptron, showed promise but were initially stymied by theoretical and practical limitations. It wasn't until the re-discovery and refinement of the backpropagation algorithm—a method for training multi-layer neural networks—that these systems began to demonstrate significant potential. Backpropagation enabled networks to learn from data in a way that mimicked, to some extent, the learning processes of biological neurons.

The reemergence of neural networks marked a turning point. Researchers began to recognize that by exposing networks to large amounts of data, they could learn complex patterns and representations without the need for explicit, hand-coded rules. This shift from symbolic reasoning to statistical learning was transformative, setting the stage for what would later be known as deep learning.

The Deep Learning Revolution

The real breakthrough in neural network research came with the advent of deep learning—a subfield of machine learning characterized by neural networks with many layers (hence "deep"). Deep learning leverages vast amounts of data and high-performance computing to train models that can automatically extract features and patterns from raw input. One of the landmark moments in this revolution occurred in 2012 with the success of AlexNet, a deep convolutional neural network that dramatically outperformed previous methods in the ImageNet Large Scale Visual Recognition Challenge. AlexNet's performance was a clear demonstration that, with the right architecture and sufficient data, neural networks could achieve unprecedented levels of accuracy in tasks like image recognition.

Since then, deep learning has rapidly advanced, becoming the backbone of many modern AI applications. From natural language processing models like GPT (Generative Pre-trained Transformer) to sophisticated computer vision systems and reinforcement learning agents, deep learning is at the core of most state-of-the-art AI technologies. Studies published in leading journals such as *Nature* and *IEEE Transactions on Neural Networks and Learning Systems* consistently highlight the exponential growth in both the capabilities and the applications of deep learning models. This exponential trajectory is fueled not only by advances in algorithm design but also by hardware improvements—GPUs and specialized AI accelerators have made it possible to train larger and more complex networks than ever before.

Foundational Technologies: Data, Hardware, and Algorithms

At the heart of the AI evolution lie three critical pillars: data, hardware, and algorithms. These elements interact synergistically to drive progress.

Data: The exponential growth of digital data has been a boon for AI. In the early days, datasets were small and painstakingly curated. Today, the internet generates terabytes of data every day, providing an almost inexhaustible resource for training machine learning models. Research has shown that the performance of deep learning models often scales with the quantity and quality of data available—an insight that has spurred the development of data-centric AI approaches. Moreover, the emergence of big data technologies has made it possible to process and analyze massive datasets in real time, further accelerating AI innovation.

Hardware: The evolution of computing hardware has been equally pivotal. The progress described by Moore's

Law—doubling the number of transistors on a chip roughly every two years—laid the groundwork for the computational explosion that supports modern AI. More recently, specialized hardware such as graphics processing units (GPUs) and tensor processing units (TPUs) have been developed specifically to accelerate machine learning workloads. These hardware advancements have enabled researchers to train deep neural networks that were once considered computationally infeasible. Studies by the Semiconductor Industry Association have highlighted how the relentless improvement in chip performance has been a critical enabler of the deep learning revolution.

Algorithms: Finally, the algorithms that underpin AI have undergone dramatic evolution. From the early, rule-based systems of the 1950s to the gradient-based learning of deep networks, the progression of AI algorithms has been marked by both incremental improvements and occasional paradigm shifts. Innovations like dropout regularization, batch normalization, and advanced optimization techniques have all contributed to making deep networks more robust and efficient. Furthermore, the development of architectures such as recurrent neural networks (RNNs), long short-term memory networks (LSTMs), and transformers has expanded the reach of AI to tasks that require an understanding of sequential data and context, such as language translation and sentiment analysis.

Bridging the Past and the Present

The evolution of artificial intelligence is a story of convergence—where ideas from neuroscience, computer science, and statistics coalesce to create systems that can learn, adapt, and ultimately transform our world. The trajectory from symbolic AI to deep learning is not merely a tale of technological progress; it is a narrative that underscores the importance of interdisciplinary thinking and the iterative nature of scientific discovery. Every breakthrough, every failure, and every subsequent refinement has brought us closer to a future where AI is not just a tool but an integral partner in shaping human endeavors.

As we reflect on this journey, it becomes clear that the evolution of AI is inextricably linked to the broader digital transformation that began in the Dot-Com Era. The spirit of experimentation, the willingness to embrace risk, and the relentless pursuit of innovation that characterized the early internet years continue to inform AI research and development today. In many ways, the AI revolution is an extension of that same entrepreneurial mindset—only now, the stakes are higher, and the potential impacts on society are even more profound.

The Road Ahead

Understanding the evolution of AI is essential not only for appreciating its current capabilities but also for anticipating its future trajectory. As we look forward, several emerging trends promise to shape the next phase of AI development. Among these are the integration of reinforcement learning with deep neural networks, the growing emphasis on unsupervised and self-supervised learning, and the exploration of hybrid models that combine symbolic reasoning with statistical learning. These advances suggest that the future of AI will be characterized by even greater flexibility, adaptability, and contextual awareness.

Moreover, as AI systems become increasingly sophisticated, the need for robust ethical frameworks and transparent governance becomes more urgent. The challenges that lie ahead are not solely technical—they are deeply human. How we choose to deploy, regulate, and integrate AI into our society will determine whether it becomes a force for widespread benefit or a source of unintended harm.

In this chapter, we have traced the remarkable evolution of artificial intelligence—from its philosophical origins and early symbolic systems, through the rise of expert systems and the neural network renaissance, to the transformative breakthroughs of deep learning. We have explored the critical roles of data, hardware, and algorithms in driving this progress, and we have seen how the legacy of early AI research continues to inform today's innovations.

The story of AI is one of continuous evolution, a journey marked by relentless curiosity and the courage to push the boundaries of what machines can do. As we move into the next chapter, we will shift our focus from the historical and technological evolution of AI to its current applications and the transformative impact it is having across industries. We will explore real-world case studies that illustrate how AI is being used to solve complex problems, reshape business models, and even redefine our notions of creativity and intelligence.

The evolution of AI is not a tale of isolated breakthroughs but a dynamic interplay of ideas, technologies, and human ambition. As we stand on the cusp of a new digital era, the lessons from the past provide both a foundation and a roadmap for the future. With a clear understanding of how far we have come, we are better equipped to navigate the challenges and seize the opportunities that lie ahead.

In the coming chapter, we embark on an exploration of today's AI landscape—a vivid, multifaceted ecosystem where cutting-edge research meets practical application. We will delve into the breakthroughs that have made headlines, the industries that are being transformed, and the societal shifts that are redefining our relationship with technology. The journey continues, and the frontier of innovation beckons us to explore the vibrant, evolving world of artificial intelligence.

Chapter 3: Today's AI Innovations – Engines of a New Revolution

From the philosophical musings of Turing to the deep neural networks that power our modern devices, the evolution of artificial intelligence has reached a vibrant, multifaceted stage. Today, AI is not confined to academic laboratories or speculative theory; it is a dynamic force transforming industries, reshaping business models, and even redefining art and creativity. In this chapter, we explore the cutting-edge innovations that are driving the current AI revolution, examining the core technologies, real-world applications, and groundbreaking case studies that illuminate how AI is changing our lives.

The Maturation of AI Technologies

Over the past decade, the rapid evolution of deep learning has ushered in a new era for AI. No longer are we limited by rudimentary pattern recognition or simplistic rule-based systems. Modern AI leverages vast neural networks, sophisticated algorithms, and unprecedented amounts of data to learn, adapt, and perform tasks that were once considered the exclusive domain of human intelligence.

At the heart of today's AI breakthroughs is deep learning, which uses layered neural networks to extract complex features from raw data. A pivotal moment in this revolution was the 2012 success of AlexNet, a deep convolutional neural network that dramatically outperformed its predecessors in the ImageNet Large Scale Visual Recognition Challenge. Since then, deep learning models have grown not only in depth and complexity but also in scope, powering everything from natural language processing to autonomous decision-making.

A study published in *Nature* demonstrated that the performance of language models has improved exponentially over recent years, with state-of-the-art systems now capable of generating human-like text. These models, such as those in the GPT series developed by OpenAI, have evolved to understand context, infer meaning, and even exhibit rudimentary forms of creativity. The advancements in these systems are supported by both increased computational power and the exponential growth in available data—a synergy that reflects the very spirit of innovation seen during the Dot-Com Era.

Generative AI: Creating New Worlds

One of the most exciting frontiers in today's AI landscape is generative AI. Unlike traditional AI systems, which are designed to classify or predict, generative models can create entirely new content—from writing poetry and composing music to generating lifelike images and even designing virtual environments. Tools like DALL-E, Midjourney, and Stable Diffusion have opened up unprecedented creative possibilities. For instance, DALL-E's ability to transform textual descriptions into detailed images is revolutionizing fields such as digital art, advertising, and even product design.

The creative potential of generative AI is underscored by its impact on industries that once relied solely on human ingenuity. In the world of fashion and design, AI is now used to forecast trends, generate design prototypes, and even create entire clothing lines with minimal human intervention. Meanwhile, in the entertainment sector, screenwriters and novelists are beginning to experiment with AI-driven brainstorming sessions, using the technology to overcome writer's block and spark new ideas.

A recent report by McKinsey & Company revealed that companies implementing AI-driven content creation have seen significant improvements in both efficiency and creative output, highlighting how these technologies are not replacing human creativity but augmenting it. This collaborative relationship between man and machine hints at a future where AI serves as a co-creator, enhancing our ability to innovate while preserving the uniquely human touch in artistic endeavors.

Transforming Traditional Industries

Beyond creative fields, AI innovations are making transformative impacts across traditional industries such as healthcare, finance, and transportation.

Healthcare:

In the realm of healthcare, AI has begun to revolutionize diagnostics, personalized medicine, and patient care. Deep learning models trained on medical images are now capable of detecting anomalies such as tumors, diabetic retinopathy, and even early signs of neurological disorders with remarkable accuracy. A study published in the *Journal of the American Medical Association* demonstrated that AI systems can match—and in some cases exceed—the diagnostic performance of human experts in interpreting radiological images. Moreover, AI-driven predictive analytics are being used to forecast disease outbreaks and optimize treatment plans, leading to more proactive and efficient healthcare delivery. These advances are not only improving patient outcomes but are also reducing costs, making high-quality care more accessible.

Finance:

The financial sector, too, has embraced AI as a tool for risk management, fraud detection, and algorithmic trading. Machine learning algorithms analyze vast streams of market data in real time, identifying patterns and making predictions that inform investment strategies. Research from the Financial Stability Board suggests that AI has the potential to enhance market efficiency and stability by mitigating systemic risks. At the same time, however, regulators are mindful of the potential pitfalls, such as the concentration of market power and the risk of automated systems amplifying market volatility. The challenge, therefore, lies in harnessing AI's capabilities while ensuring that robust safeguards and ethical frameworks are in place.

Transportation:

Autonomous vehicles represent one of the most visible and transformative applications of AI in transportation. Companies like Tesla, Waymo, and Cruise are developing self-driving cars that rely on a fusion of deep learning, sensor fusion, and real-time data analysis to navigate complex environments safely. A study by the National Highway Traffic Safety Administration has suggested that widespread adoption of autonomous vehicles could dramatically reduce accidents caused by human error, potentially saving thousands of lives each year. Furthermore, the integration of AI in transportation logistics is optimizing supply chains, reducing fuel consumption, and even reimagining urban planning as cities evolve to accommodate these new technologies.

The AI Ecosystem: Collaboration and Competition

The development of today's AI innovations is characterized by a complex ecosystem where collaboration and competition coexist. On one hand, open-source communities and academic research have played a critical role in driving progress. Platforms like TensorFlow and PyTorch have democratized access to powerful AI tools, enabling researchers and developers around the world to contribute to and build upon existing work. This open collaboration has accelerated innovation and helped create a shared knowledge base that benefits the entire field.

On the other hand, fierce competition among tech giants has spurred rapid advancements, particularly in commercial applications. Companies like Google, Microsoft, and Amazon invest billions in AI research, striving to outpace one another in developing systems that can drive new revenue streams and capture emerging markets. While this competition can lead to rapid innovation, it also raises important questions about the concentration of power and the ethical use of AI. Recent debates around data privacy, algorithmic bias, and the accountability of AI systems underscore the need for transparent and responsible practices as the technology continues to mature.

The Human Element: Trust, Transparency, and Ethical AI

Amid these technological breakthroughs, one of the most pressing challenges is ensuring that AI systems are designed and deployed in ways that are ethical, transparent, and aligned with human values. As AI becomes more deeply integrated into our lives, trust becomes paramount. For instance, research published in *IEEE Transactions on Neural Networks and Learning Systems* emphasizes that explainable AI—systems that can provide clear, interpretable insights into their decision-making processes—is essential for building and maintaining public trust.

Ethical AI is not just a technical challenge; it is a societal imperative. The deployment of AI in sensitive areas such as healthcare, criminal justice, and financial services demands that we carefully consider issues of fairness, accountability, and transparency. Initiatives such as the Partnership on AI and guidelines from the European Commission aim to address these concerns by establishing ethical frameworks and regulatory standards that can guide the development and application of AI technologies.

Moreover, interdisciplinary research is playing a crucial role in bridging the gap between technological capability and ethical practice. Studies in cognitive science, philosophy, and sociology are increasingly informing AI development, ensuring that the systems we build are not only powerful but also respectful of human dignity and autonomy. This integrative approach is vital for realizing the full potential of AI while safeguarding against unintended consequences.

Real-World Case Studies: Successes and Lessons Learned

To illustrate the transformative impact of today's AI innovations, consider several real-world case studies that showcase both success and the challenges that remain.

One compelling example comes from the field of natural language processing. OpenAI's GPT series, particularly the most recent iterations, have demonstrated remarkable abilities in generating coherent, contextually relevant text. These models are used in a wide array of applications—from chatbots and virtual assistants to content creation and translation services. Their success is underpinned by the sheer scale of data and computational power available today, a stark contrast to the modest beginnings of early AI systems. Yet, as researchers have noted, these models are not without their flaws, such as biases in training data and occasional lapses in factual accuracy. Addressing these issues remains a critical focus for ongoing research.

In healthcare, deep learning has made significant strides in improving diagnostic accuracy. For example, AI systems deployed in hospitals have been shown to detect diabetic retinopathy—a leading cause of blindness—at rates comparable to expert ophthalmologists. These successes highlight the potential for AI to augment human expertise and transform patient care. However, they also underscore the importance of rigorous clinical validation and the need to integrate AI tools into existing healthcare workflows seamlessly.

Another instructive case comes from the realm of autonomous vehicles. Companies developing self-driving technology have faced a steep learning curve, balancing the promise of reduced traffic accidents and increased mobility against the challenges of navigating unpredictable real-world environments. Incidents involving autonomous vehicles, while statistically rare, have sparked intense debate about safety standards and regulatory oversight. These experiences provide valuable lessons on the importance of robust testing, public transparency, and the incremental rollout of new technologies.

Transitioning to the Future

The innovations discussed in this chapter are more than just technological marvels—they are the building blocks of a new digital ecosystem that is reshaping our world. As we have seen, the rapid advancements in deep learning, generative AI, and other core technologies are driving transformative changes across industries. The AI revolution, much like the Dot-Com Era before it, is characterized by a spirit of relentless innovation and the willingness to embrace both the opportunities and challenges that come with disruptive change.

Yet, as we celebrate these achievements, we must also remain vigilant. The promise of AI is immense, but so too are the risks. Balancing innovation with ethical responsibility, competition with collaboration, and technical progress with societal impact will be crucial as we navigate this uncharted territory. The lessons of the Dot-Com Era—its triumphs, its failures, and the enduring legacy of its entrepreneurial spirit—offer a valuable roadmap for managing the complexities of today's AI landscape.

As we prepare to move forward, the next chapter will take us deeper into the practical applications of AI. We will explore how AI is being integrated into various sectors, the challenges of scaling these innovations, and the role of governance in shaping an AI-enabled future. By understanding not only the technologies themselves but also the human and institutional dynamics at play, we can better envision a future where AI serves as a tool for empowerment and progress.

In closing this chapter, we see that today's AI innovations are the engines driving a new revolution—one that is as much about human ingenuity and ethical stewardship as it is about raw computational power. The transition from early research breakthroughs to real-world applications is an ongoing journey, marked by both exhilarating successes and sobering challenges. With these insights in mind, our exploration of the AI revolution continues as we now turn our focus to the transformative impact of AI on our industries, our work, and our society. The next chapter will delve into these real-world applications, drawing on case studies and personal narratives to illustrate how AI is reshaping our present and setting the stage for the future.

Chapter 4: Beyond Today – Envisioning the Future of AI

As we stand at the precipice of technological transformation, it is impossible to ignore the horizon of possibilities that lie beyond today's achievements. While the evolution of artificial intelligence has already redefined industries and reshaped everyday life, the future promises an even more radical convergence of human ingenuity and machine capability. In this chapter, we venture into the realms of emerging technologies and visionary applications that signal the next phase of the AI revolution. By examining current research trends, forecasting future breakthroughs, and reflecting on interdisciplinary insights, we can begin to chart a path toward a future where AI not only augments human potential but also redefines the very nature of our existence.

Uncharted Territories: The Next Paradigm Shifts

Historically, each major leap in technology has been marked by the emergence of a paradigm shift—a new way of thinking that overturns old assumptions and paves the way for unimagined possibilities. The Dot-Com Era and the deep learning revolution have both exemplified this phenomenon. Today, several nascent fields promise to ignite the next wave of transformative change in artificial intelligence.

One area garnering significant attention is quantum computing. Unlike classical computers, which perform calculations in a linear, step-by-step fashion, quantum computers leverage the principles of superposition and entanglement to process vast amounts of data simultaneously. Researchers at institutions such as IBM and Google have already demonstrated quantum supremacy in controlled experiments, and although practical, large-scale quantum computing remains a work in progress, its potential to accelerate AI is enormous. Studies published in journals like *Nature* suggest that quantum algorithms could dramatically reduce the time required to solve optimization problems and simulate complex systems—tasks that currently limit the capabilities of classical AI models. In a future where quantum computing becomes accessible, the computational bottlenecks that constrain deep learning could be shattered, unlocking new levels of efficiency and problem-solving prowess.

Convergence of AI with Emerging Technologies

The future of AI is not solely a story of more powerful algorithms; it is also one of convergence—where artificial intelligence integrates seamlessly with other emerging technologies to create systems that are adaptive, autonomous, and deeply interconnected. Consider the Internet of Things (IoT), which envisions a world where billions of devices communicate in real time. When AI meets IoT, the result is a network of "smart" objects capable of learning from their environment and collaborating to optimize everything from energy usage in smart cities to predictive maintenance in industrial settings.

For example, in the realm of smart cities, AI-driven sensors and data analytics platforms are already being piloted to improve traffic management, reduce energy consumption, and enhance public safety. A study by the International Data Corporation (IDC) forecasts that the global smart city market could be worth over $2 trillion by 2025, driven largely by advancements in AI and IoT integration. In this future, everyday infrastructure—from streetlights to public transportation—will be embedded with intelligent systems that anticipate needs and dynamically adapt to changing conditions, creating more resilient and responsive urban environments.

Another significant convergence is that of AI with biotechnology and neuroscience. The concept of brain–machine interfaces (BMIs) has long been the stuff of science fiction, but recent breakthroughs have brought us closer to the reality of direct neural integration. Companies like Neuralink are working to develop implantable devices that can facilitate real-time communication between the human brain and computers. Such technologies could revolutionize healthcare by enabling treatments for neurological disorders, restoring lost sensory functions, or even augmenting human cognition. Moreover, as AI algorithms learn to interpret neural signals more accurately, the boundary between biological and artificial intelligence will blur further—raising profound questions about identity, autonomy, and what it means to be human.

Ethical Horizons and Governance Challenges

With every new technological frontier comes a host of ethical and regulatory challenges. The unprecedented capabilities of AI, especially when coupled with quantum computing or neural integration, demand that we rethink not only the mechanics of innovation but also its moral underpinnings. Recent surveys by the Pew Research Center have shown that public concern about AI's impact on employment, privacy, and societal well-being is at an all-time high. While many of these concerns are reminiscent of those raised during the Dot-Com Era, the stakes are now far greater.

One promising approach to addressing these challenges is the development of explainable AI (XAI)—systems that not only perform tasks efficiently but also provide clear, interpretable insights into their decision-making processes. A study published in *IEEE Transactions on*

Neural Networks and Learning Systems underscores the importance of XAI in building trust and accountability. As AI systems grow more complex, ensuring that their operations are transparent becomes critical for both regulatory oversight and public confidence. The implementation of ethical frameworks, such as those proposed by the European Commission's AI guidelines, is already setting the stage for responsible AI development. However, as we push further into uncharted territories, it will be essential to foster global cooperation and interdisciplinary dialogue to craft policies that can keep pace with rapid innovation.

Visions of an AI-Enabled Future

Looking ahead, several visionary scenarios offer tantalizing glimpses into what an AI-enabled future might look like. One such scenario is the concept of ubiquitous personal AI assistants—intelligent systems that seamlessly integrate with every aspect of our daily lives. Imagine an AI that not only manages your schedule and finances but also anticipates your needs, provides personalized education, and even helps maintain your health through real-time monitoring and intervention. A recent report by Gartner projects that by 2030, personal AI assistants could become as common as smartphones, fundamentally altering the way we interact with technology.

Another compelling vision is that of AI-driven creative collaboration. While current generative AI models are already producing impressive works of art, music, and literature, the future may hold even more profound possibilities. Consider a world where artists and writers work side by side with AI systems, each learning from the other to push the boundaries of creativity. Studies from the MIT Media Lab suggest that such human–AI collaborations can lead to novel forms of artistic expression and innovation that neither could achieve alone. In this future, AI is not a substitute for human creativity but an extension of it—a tool that amplifies our creative capacities and helps us explore new realms of expression.

Perhaps one of the most transformative possibilities lies in the integration of AI with sustainable technologies. As concerns about climate change and environmental degradation intensify, AI can play a critical role in optimizing resource management, reducing waste, and promoting renewable energy solutions. For instance, AI-driven analytics are already being used to optimize energy grids, predict equipment failures in wind turbines, and even design more efficient solar panels. Research by the International Energy Agency (IEA) indicates that AI could help reduce global energy consumption by up to 10% by 2040, a reduction that would have profound implications for sustainability and environmental conservation.

Navigating the Complexities of the Future

As we envision these future scenarios, it is important to acknowledge that the path forward is not without its uncertainties. The rapid pace of innovation means that predictions, no matter how well-informed, are subject to the whims of technological progress and unforeseen societal shifts. The lessons of the past—the exuberance, the bust, and the eventual recalibration of the Dot-Com Era—remind us that transformation is an iterative process. It involves not only groundbreaking discoveries but also moments of reflection, adjustment, and sometimes, painful course corrections.

A significant body of research, including insights from the World Economic Forum and various academic institutions, emphasizes that managing this transition will require an agile and adaptive approach. Policymakers, business leaders, and technologists must work in tandem to develop frameworks that are both flexible and robust—capable of accommodating rapid change while safeguarding public interests. Interdisciplinary collaboration will be key, as the challenges posed by advanced AI extend beyond the confines of computer science and into the realms of ethics, sociology, and governance.

Preparing for a New Era: Strategies for Success

The vision of a future powered by AI is both exhilarating and daunting. To navigate this landscape successfully, we must cultivate a mindset that embraces continuous learning, resilience, and ethical foresight. Entrepreneurs and innovators can draw inspiration from the pioneering spirit of the Dot-Com Era—its willingness to take risks, its capacity for rapid iteration, and its enduring commitment to challenging the status quo. At the same time, the future demands a more nuanced approach, one that balances ambition with responsibility.

For businesses, this means investing in talent, fostering a culture of innovation, and adopting practices that prioritize both growth and ethical considerations. Research from McKinsey has shown that companies that successfully integrate AI into their operations not only achieve operational efficiencies but also gain a competitive edge by anticipating market shifts and consumer needs. In parallel, educational institutions and governments must collaborate to ensure that the workforce is equipped with the skills needed to thrive in an AI-driven economy. This may involve rethinking traditional educational models, promoting lifelong learning, and investing in retraining programs to help workers transition to new roles.

A Collaborative Future: Building Bridges Across Disciplines

Perhaps the most promising aspect of this journey toward the future is the growing recognition of the need for collaboration across disciplines. The most significant breakthroughs in AI are emerging from the confluence of diverse fields—where insights from neuroscience, physics, economics, and ethics converge to inspire innovative solutions. This interdisciplinary approach is already visible in initiatives like the Partnership on AI, which brings together experts from academia, industry, and civil society to address the multifaceted challenges of AI development.

As we look forward, this collaborative spirit must become a cornerstone of our strategy. It is only by working together—across sectors, across borders, and across disciplines—that we can hope to harness the full potential of AI while mitigating its risks. Such cooperation will be essential for creating regulatory frameworks that are both forward-looking and inclusive, ensuring that the benefits of AI are distributed equitably across society.

In this chapter, we have journeyed beyond today's achievements and ventured into the realm of future possibilities—a world where AI, in concert with emerging technologies, promises to reshape our lives in profound and unexpected ways. We have explored the transformative potential of quantum computing, IoT integration, brain–machine interfaces, and sustainable technologies, each offering a glimpse of a future where technology is not merely a tool but a partner in human progress.

At the same time, we have acknowledged the challenges that lie ahead—ethical dilemmas, regulatory uncertainties, and the need for an adaptive, interdisciplinary approach. The lessons of the past and the innovations of the present converge to create a roadmap for the future—one that requires us to balance ambition with responsibility and innovation with thoughtful oversight.

As we prepare to transition into the next phase of our exploration, the focus will shift from visionary predictions to the practical realities of AI's impact on society. The forthcoming chapters will delve into case studies and personal narratives that illustrate how AI is already transforming industries such as healthcare, finance, transportation, and creative arts. We will examine the real-world applications of AI, the challenges of scaling these innovations, and the role of governance in shaping a future that is as ethical as it is groundbreaking.

The future of AI is not a distant, abstract concept—it is unfolding before our eyes, layer by layer, system by system. With the foundational insights of today and the lessons gleaned from past revolutions in hand, we are better equipped to navigate the complexities of this new era. In the next chapter, we will take a closer look at how these theoretical advancements are being put into practice, and how they are beginning to redefine the fabric of our society. The journey into the practical applications of AI awaits, promising both opportunities for growth and challenges that will test our collective ingenuity.

Chapter 5: Ethical Frontiers and Governance in the AI Age

In the exhilarating rush of innovation, where algorithms scale new heights and deep learning models break records, it is easy to be captivated solely by the technical marvels of artificial intelligence. Yet as AI systems become increasingly powerful and ubiquitous, they inevitably raise profound ethical questions and governance challenges that must be addressed if technology is to serve humanity's best interests. This chapter delves into the ethical frontiers of AI—exploring issues of bias, transparency, accountability, and the broader societal impacts of intelligent systems—and examines the evolving frameworks for regulating and guiding AI development.

The Ethical Imperative in a Rapidly Evolving Landscape

AI has transformed industries and redefined possibilities, but its rapid progress also amplifies ethical risks. One of the most pressing concerns is that AI systems, often perceived as neutral tools, can inadvertently perpetuate and even exacerbate biases embedded in their training data. Numerous studies, such as those featured in *IEEE Transactions on Neural Networks and Learning Systems*, have documented cases where facial recognition algorithms perform significantly worse on minority populations compared to their performance on majority groups. Such disparities not only undermine the reliability of AI but also risk deepening existing social inequalities.

Beyond bias, transparency in AI decision-making has emerged as a critical ethical issue. As models grow in complexity, the "black box" problem—where the rationale behind an AI's decisions remains opaque—presents a significant barrier to trust and accountability. For example, when an AI system is used in judicial sentencing or loan approvals, understanding how it arrived at a particular decision is essential for ensuring fairness. This has led to a burgeoning field known as explainable AI (XAI), which seeks to develop models that are not only effective but also interpretable by humans. The drive for transparency is not merely technical; it is a moral imperative that ensures individuals affected by AI decisions can challenge and understand those outcomes.

Accountability and the Role of Regulation

The question of accountability in AI systems is multifaceted. Who is responsible when an AI system causes harm—be it a misdiagnosis in healthcare, a biased hiring decision, or a malfunctioning autonomous vehicle?

Traditional legal frameworks, developed long before the advent of AI, struggle to assign liability in cases where decisions result from the interplay of complex algorithms, vast datasets, and human oversight. As a consequence, regulators around the world are racing to develop new standards that can keep pace with the technological revolution.

The European Commission's guidelines on trustworthy AI provide one example of early efforts to codify ethical principles into actionable policy. These guidelines emphasize four core requirements for AI systems: respect for human autonomy, prevention of harm, fairness, and explicability. Such frameworks serve as a starting point for more robust regulatory measures, aiming to ensure that as AI systems become more autonomous and influential, they are designed with a fundamental commitment to protecting individual rights and societal well-being.

Recent work by the Future of Life Institute and other advocacy groups underscores the need for proactive regulation. Their calls for "pause" periods in the development of particularly potent AI systems reflect a cautious approach—a recognition that unchecked technological progress could lead to unforeseen, and potentially irreversible, societal impacts. The challenge lies in striking a delicate balance: fostering an environment that encourages innovation while ensuring that robust ethical and legal safeguards are in place.

Global Cooperation and Interdisciplinary Collaboration

No single nation or corporation can address the ethical challenges of AI in isolation. The technology's global reach and transformative potential demand an international, collaborative approach. Multi-stakeholder initiatives such as the Partnership on AI and the Global Partnership on AI bring together researchers, industry leaders, policymakers, and civil society representatives from around the world to develop shared standards and best practices. These collaborative efforts are crucial for establishing a level playing field, preventing a regulatory race to the bottom, and ensuring that AI development is aligned with universal human values.

Interdisciplinary research is also playing a vital role in bridging the gap between technical advancements and ethical imperatives. Scholars from fields as diverse as cognitive science, philosophy, sociology, and law are contributing insights that enrich our understanding of how AI impacts human life. For instance, philosophical investigations into the nature of consciousness and moral agency provide a conceptual framework for discussing machine ethics and the potential rights of intelligent systems. Simultaneously, sociological studies reveal how technology influences social dynamics and power structures. This confluence of perspectives is not only broadening the discourse but is also laying the groundwork for more holistic governance models that can anticipate and address the multifaceted challenges posed by AI.

The Social Impact of AI: A Double-Edged Sword

While AI holds immense promise for improving efficiency, driving innovation, and enhancing quality of life, its social impact is not uniformly positive. The deployment of AI in areas such as employment, healthcare, and law enforcement has sparked heated debates about its potential to both empower and disenfranchise individuals.

Consider the impact on employment. Studies by the World Economic Forum suggest that AI and automation could displace millions of jobs over the next decade, particularly in sectors reliant on routine, repetitive tasks. However, these same studies also predict that new roles—often requiring advanced technical or creative skills—will emerge. The transition, therefore, poses a significant challenge: how do we prepare a workforce for an era where the nature of work is fundamentally altered? The answer may lie in robust educational reforms, reskilling initiatives, and social safety nets that ensure the benefits of AI-driven growth are widely shared.

In the realm of healthcare, AI systems have the potential to democratize access to diagnostic and therapeutic services, particularly in underserved communities. Yet, the deployment of AI in clinical settings also raises issues of privacy, consent, and the equitable distribution of care. For example, while AI-driven diagnostic tools can rapidly analyze medical images with high accuracy, they must also be designed to protect sensitive patient data and operate without perpetuating biases that could lead to unequal treatment.

The use of AI in law enforcement and public safety further illustrates the complexity of its social impact. Surveillance systems powered by AI can enhance security and deter crime, but they also risk encroaching on civil liberties and exacerbating issues of discrimination. The challenge for policymakers is to harness the benefits of AI while instituting strict oversight to prevent abuses—ensuring that security measures do not come at the expense of personal freedom and justice.

Ethical Frameworks for the Future

As we look toward a future where AI becomes increasingly autonomous and integrated into every aspect of society, the need for comprehensive ethical frameworks has never been more pressing. These frameworks must go beyond abstract principles to provide concrete guidelines for the design, deployment, and governance of AI systems. One promising approach is the concept of "value-sensitive design," which advocates for the integration of ethical considerations into the very fabric of technological development. By engaging diverse stakeholders—including ethicists, end-users, and affected communities—in the design process, developers can create systems that are not only technically robust but also socially responsible.

Furthermore, regulatory bodies must be agile enough to adapt to rapid technological change. Traditional legislative processes, which often move slowly in the face of fast-paced innovation, may need to be supplemented with new mechanisms for real-time oversight and dynamic rulemaking. Concepts such as regulatory sandboxes—controlled environments where new technologies can be tested under the watchful eye of regulators—offer one potential solution. These experimental frameworks can help identify potential risks and refine standards before widespread deployment, ensuring that new technologies are introduced in a manner that is both innovative and safe.

Preparing Society for a Transformed Future

Ultimately, the ethical and governance challenges of AI extend beyond the realm of technology—they are about how we choose to shape our collective future. The decisions made today will have far-reaching implications for generations to come. It is not enough for technologists and policymakers to focus solely on the technical aspects of AI; we must also engage in a broader societal dialogue about the kind of future we want to build. This means rethinking our economic models, our educational systems, and even our cultural narratives to ensure that the benefits of AI are equitably distributed and that no one is left behind in the digital transformation.

Public education and awareness are critical components of this endeavor. As AI systems become more integrated into our lives, individuals must be empowered with the knowledge and skills to navigate this new landscape. Initiatives aimed at improving digital literacy, fostering ethical awareness, and encouraging civic participation will play a crucial role in preparing society for the challenges and opportunities of an AI-enabled world.

Conclusion and Transition

In this chapter, we have journeyed through the ethical frontiers and governance challenges that accompany the rapid advancement of artificial intelligence. From addressing issues of bias, transparency, and accountability to forging collaborative frameworks that span national and disciplinary boundaries, the path toward ethical AI is both complex and imperative. The lessons from the Dot-Com Era—where unchecked innovation eventually gave way to a more measured, sustainable approach—offer valuable insights for managing the transformative potential of AI.

As we move forward, the focus must increasingly shift from technical breakthroughs to the human and societal dimensions of AI. The ethical dilemmas we face today are not mere obstacles; they are opportunities to reimagine how technology can serve the greater good. By embedding ethical principles into the core of AI development and governance, we can pave the way for a future where innovation and responsibility go hand in hand.

Our exploration of AI's ethical landscape is far from complete. In the next chapter, we will turn our attention to the entrepreneurial ecosystem surrounding AI—examining how startups, established companies, and investors are navigating the balance between risk and opportunity. We will delve into case studies that illustrate how innovative business models are leveraging AI to drive growth, as well as the challenges they face in scaling these technologies responsibly. This next phase of our journey will shed light on the practical strategies that are shaping the future of technology-driven enterprise, continuing our exploration of how humanity can harness the power of AI for transformative, positive change.

Thus, as we conclude our discussion on ethical frontiers, the conversation seamlessly transitions into a deep dive into the dynamic interplay of entrepreneurship and innovation in the AI era—a story of vision, resilience, and the relentless pursuit of a better tomorrow.

Chapter 6: The Entrepreneurial Ecosystem – AI Startups and Investment Trends

In the dynamic landscape of artificial intelligence, innovation is not solely the domain of research labs and academic journals—it is also fueled by an entrepreneurial spirit that thrives in the unpredictable realm of startups and venture capital. Just as the Dot-Com Era was characterized by a fervent burst of entrepreneurial energy and risk-taking, today's AI ecosystem is witnessing a similar phenomenon, albeit on an even more expansive and transformative scale. In this chapter, we explore the vibrant entrepreneurial ecosystem that is propelling the AI revolution, the investment trends that are shaping its future, and the lessons learned from past technological booms that are helping to steer this new era toward sustainable growth.

The Rise of AI Startups: A New Breed of Innovators

The story of AI entrepreneurship is one of relentless optimism and bold risk-taking. In recent years, AI startups have emerged as key players in the tech world, attracting massive amounts of venture capital and reshaping entire industries. Unlike traditional companies that have gradually integrated AI into their operations, these startups are built from the ground up with AI at their core. They are designed to solve complex problems using data-driven insights, often disrupting conventional business models in the process.

These startups operate in a landscape marked by fierce competition and rapid innovation. Many are founded by teams of young, ambitious entrepreneurs who have honed their skills in academic research or at established tech giants. They enter the market with a unique combination of technical expertise, creative vision, and a willingness to challenge the status quo. This new breed of innovators is driven by a belief that AI is not just a tool for incremental improvement, but a transformative force capable of reshaping entire sectors—from healthcare and finance to agriculture and entertainment.

A recent report by CB Insights highlighted that AI startups have grown at an unprecedented pace, with investments surging by over 300% in the past few years. This growth is not just a testament to the potential of AI but also an indicator of the high level of confidence that investors have in the technology's ability to deliver groundbreaking solutions. Entrepreneurs are seizing this moment to build companies that not only capture market share but also redefine what is possible in the digital age.

Venture Capital and the Funding Frenzy

The engine that drives the entrepreneurial ecosystem is venture capital—a source of funding that has proven indispensable for high-risk, high-reward ventures. In the world of AI, venture capitalists are not only betting on technology; they are betting on people—on visionary founders who can translate complex algorithms into practical applications that meet real-world needs.

Investment trends in AI reveal a landscape that is both exciting and fiercely competitive. Major firms like Sequoia Capital, Andreessen Horowitz, and SoftBank have been at the forefront, funneling billions of dollars into startups that promise to revolutionize industries. These investors are looking for companies with the potential to scale rapidly, create new markets, and ultimately become the next generation of tech giants.

However, the influx of capital is a double-edged sword. While it provides the resources necessary for innovation and rapid growth, it also creates immense pressure on startups to deliver results quickly. This pressure can sometimes lead to a "growth at all costs" mentality, where the focus on rapid expansion overshadows the need for robust, sustainable business models. The lessons from the Dot-Com Era—where exuberant growth was often followed by catastrophic collapse—serve as a cautionary tale for today's AI investors.

To navigate these challenges, many investors are adopting a more measured approach, emphasizing due diligence, long-term vision, and an understanding of the ethical and societal implications of the technologies they support. Regulatory bodies and industry groups are also beginning to weigh in, advocating for frameworks that balance innovation with accountability. The goal is to foster an environment where AI startups can thrive without succumbing to the pitfalls of unchecked growth and speculation.

Business Models and the Path to Sustainability

The entrepreneurial journey in AI is not solely about technological breakthroughs—it is equally about developing sustainable business models that can withstand the test of time. Successful AI startups understand that technology is only as valuable as the solutions it provides to pressing problems. They focus on building products and services that address real-world needs, whether it's through improving diagnostic accuracy in healthcare, optimizing supply chains in logistics, or personalizing customer experiences in retail.

For instance, consider the example of an AI-driven healthcare startup that uses deep learning algorithms to analyze medical images. Initially, the technology might capture headlines for its impressive diagnostic capabilities, but its long-term success will depend on its integration into clinical workflows, its ability to maintain regulatory compliance, and its effectiveness in reducing costs and improving patient outcomes. This requires a delicate balance of technical innovation, operational excellence, and customer-centric design.

A study published by McKinsey & Company has shown that companies that successfully integrate AI into their core business processes not only see significant improvements in efficiency but also achieve a competitive edge in their markets. These companies are characterized by their ability to iterate quickly, adapt to changing market conditions, and continuously refine their business models based on customer feedback and technological advancements.

Entrepreneurs in the AI space are increasingly aware of these dynamics. They are moving away from the notion of "disruption for disruption's sake" and focusing instead on building scalable, resilient businesses that can deliver sustainable value over the long term. This shift is partly driven by the maturity of the technology and partly by the evolving expectations of investors and consumers, who now demand more than just visionary ideas—they want tangible results and reliable performance.

The Intersection of Innovation and Regulation

As AI startups continue to push the boundaries of what is possible, the role of regulation becomes ever more critical. The challenges posed by advanced AI systems—ranging from data privacy and security to algorithmic fairness and transparency—demand that entrepreneurs work closely with regulators to create an ecosystem that is both innovative and responsible.

Recent initiatives, such as the European Union's General Data Protection Regulation (GDPR) and the forthcoming AI Act, highlight the growing recognition that robust regulatory frameworks are essential for protecting public interests while fostering technological advancement. These regulations are designed to ensure that AI systems are developed and deployed in ways that are ethical, transparent, and accountable. For startups, navigating this regulatory landscape is both a challenge and an opportunity. By building compliance into their operations from the outset, they can not only mitigate risks but also gain a competitive advantage by positioning themselves as trustworthy, responsible players in the market.

Moreover, regulatory environments are becoming more collaborative, with public and private sectors working together to set standards and share best practices. Industry consortia and advisory groups, such as the Partnership on AI, play a pivotal role in shaping these policies, ensuring that the rapid pace of innovation does not come at the expense of ethical considerations or social welfare.

Challenges and Opportunities in a Global Marketplace

The global nature of the AI revolution means that startups and investors must also contend with the complexities of international markets. Different regions have varying levels of regulatory maturity, technological infrastructure, and cultural attitudes toward innovation. For example, while Silicon Valley remains a powerhouse of AI entrepreneurship, emerging markets in Asia, Europe, and Latin America are quickly catching up, driven by localized innovations and tailored business models.

A report by the International Data Corporation (IDC) projects that global spending on AI will exceed $500 billion by 2024, a clear indication that the race for AI dominance is truly international. This global competition presents both challenges and opportunities. On the one hand, startups must navigate diverse regulatory environments, competitive pressures, and the logistical challenges of scaling across borders. On the other hand, access to a global talent pool, combined with international collaboration and market diversity, can accelerate innovation and drive more robust, resilient business models.

Entrepreneurs who succeed in this global marketplace will be those who can adapt their strategies to local contexts while maintaining a clear, unified vision. They will need to build organizations that are agile, culturally sensitive, and capable of operating in a rapidly evolving technological landscape. The interplay between global competition and local adaptation is a key factor in the long-term success of AI startups.

The Human Side of Entrepreneurship

Behind every successful AI startup is a story of passion, perseverance, and relentless drive. The entrepreneurial journey is as much about the people as it is about the technology. Founders, engineers, and investors alike share a common belief in the transformative power of AI—a belief that motivates them to push through challenges, learn from failures, and continuously innovate. Their stories are filled with moments of inspiration and instances of hard-won breakthroughs, each one contributing to the rich tapestry of the AI revolution.

Personal narratives and case studies offer valuable insights into what it takes to succeed in this high-stakes environment. Many AI entrepreneurs recount their early days of grappling with limited resources, fierce competition, and the inherent uncertainty of pioneering uncharted territory. They describe the exhilaration of a breakthrough moment—the sudden realization that a complex algorithm finally works, or that a prototype is ready for market testing. These moments, however fleeting, are the fuel that sustains long-term innovation and drive the ecosystem forward.

Moreover, the culture of mentorship and collaboration that has emerged in the tech community plays a critical role in supporting new ventures. Experienced entrepreneurs and investors often serve as mentors, offering guidance, resources, and strategic insights to help navigate the turbulent waters of startup life. This culture of support not only accelerates individual success but also contributes to a more vibrant, resilient entrepreneurial ecosystem overall.

Preparing for the Future: Strategies for Growth and Resilience

As we look ahead, the challenges and opportunities for AI startups are both immense and multifaceted. To thrive in this environment, entrepreneurs must cultivate a mindset that embraces change, values continuous learning, and prioritizes both innovation and ethical responsibility. Strategic investments in talent, technology, and partnerships are essential for scaling operations and driving sustainable growth.

Educational initiatives and training programs are also critical. As AI continues to evolve, the demand for skilled professionals who can bridge the gap between technical expertise and business acumen is growing. Universities, online platforms, and corporate training programs are stepping up to meet this demand, ensuring that the next generation of innovators is well-equipped to drive the future of AI.

At the same time, entrepreneurs must remain vigilant about the risks associated with rapid growth. The lessons of the Dot-Com Era remind us that unchecked ambition can lead to unsustainable practices and eventual collapse. By adopting a balanced approach—one that values both agility and prudence—startups can build resilient organizations capable of weathering market fluctuations and evolving challenges.

Transitioning to the Next Phase

In this chapter, we have explored the entrepreneurial ecosystem that underpins the AI revolution—an ecosystem characterized by bold vision, fierce competition, and a relentless drive to innovate. We have seen how venture capital, global market dynamics, and the human element converge to create a fertile ground for groundbreaking ideas and transformative technologies. The journey of AI startups is one of both extraordinary opportunity and significant challenge, requiring a delicate balance of ambition, discipline, and ethical stewardship.

As we prepare to transition to the next phase of our exploration, the focus will shift from the business dynamics of AI to the cultural and societal implications of these technological advancements. In the forthcoming chapter, we will delve into the profound ways in which AI is reshaping our society—altering how we interact, work, and even think. We will examine the broader impact of AI on social structures, individual identities, and the very fabric of our communities. Through personal narratives, case studies, and interdisciplinary insights, we will explore how this digital revolution is influencing our collective future.

The entrepreneurial spirit that has driven AI innovation is not isolated from its cultural context. In fact, the same forces that propel startups to disrupt traditional industries are also reshaping our social interactions and expectations. As AI continues to permeate every aspect of our lives, it challenges us to redefine what it means to be human in a digital age. How do we maintain our individuality, creativity, and ethical standards in the face of algorithms that can mimic and even surpass human capabilities?

This delicate balance—between technological advancement and human values—lies at the heart of the ongoing digital transformation. The entrepreneurial ecosystem provides a powerful engine for innovation, but it also raises critical questions about equity, access, and the societal impact of disruptive technologies. As we turn our attention to the cultural dimensions of the AI revolution in the next chapter, we will build on the insights gained here about how startups and investors are not only shaping industries but also influencing the broader narrative of our time.

Thus, as we close this chapter on the entrepreneurial landscape of AI, we carry forward a rich tapestry of lessons—from the raw ambition and rapid growth of startups to the strategic foresight needed for sustainable success. These insights form the bedrock upon which we will examine the societal and cultural shifts that AI is engendering in our next exploration. The journey of innovation is far from over; it is an ongoing narrative that weaves together technology, business, and humanity into an ever-evolving story of progress and possibility.

Chapter 7: Culture, Creativity, and the New Digital Identity

In our journey through the evolution and impact of artificial intelligence—from its humble origins to its transformative applications in industry and entrepreneurship—we now turn our attention to a dimension that is as profound as it is personal: culture. Today's AI revolution is not just a story of algorithms and hardware; it is also a narrative about how technology reshapes our identity, creativity, and the way we connect with one another. This chapter explores the cultural shifts emerging in the wake of AI, the ways in which our digital identities are being redefined, and how creative expression is being transformed by intelligent systems.

The Shifting Landscape of Digital Culture

The digital age has always been a catalyst for cultural change. In the early days of the internet, the Dot-Com Era sparked an explosion of new forms of expression and social interaction. Websites, blogs, and early social media platforms reconfigured how people shared information, built communities, and expressed themselves. Today, AI is taking that evolution to a new level. Intelligent systems are no longer passive tools; they are active participants in the cultural dialogue, influencing everything from art and literature to the way we perceive ourselves and our communities.

One of the most significant cultural shifts is the way AI is reshaping our digital identities. In the past, our online personas were largely curated through static profiles, carefully crafted messages, and the selective sharing of personal information. Now, with the advent of advanced machine learning algorithms and data analytics, our digital identities are becoming dynamic, multi-layered, and even predictive. Social media platforms use AI to analyze our behavior and preferences, tailoring content in ways that reinforce certain aspects of our identity—even as they obscure others. A study by the Pew Research Center found that a growing number of users feel that algorithms "know them better than they know themselves," highlighting a trend where technology begins to shape self-perception.

AI as a Creative Collaborator

In the realm of creative expression, AI is emerging as a collaborator, muse, and even a co-creator. Gone are the days when technology was relegated to the background of art; today, AI is at the forefront of creative innovation. Tools like generative adversarial networks (GANs) and natural language models have made it possible to produce art, music, and literature that are not only aesthetically compelling but also intellectually provocative. These AI-generated works challenge our understanding of creativity, raising questions about authorship and originality.

Take, for instance, the recent surge of AI art exhibits where algorithms create intricate, unexpected visuals based on patterns learned from thousands of works. Artists are now using AI not merely as a tool but as a partner in the creative process. In one notable case, a collaborative project between human artists and AI resulted in a multimedia installation that blended traditional painting techniques with digital imagery—a work that invited viewers to explore the interplay between human intuition and machine precision. Critics have noted that such projects push the boundaries of conventional art forms and encourage us to rethink what it means to be creative in the 21st century.

Similarly, in music, AI composers are experimenting with sounds and structures that transcend the familiar. Platforms like OpenAI's MuseNet and Jukebox can generate compositions that span multiple genres and styles, offering a glimpse into a future where music is continuously reimagined. These AI-driven creations do not replace human musicians; rather, they serve as catalysts for new forms of musical dialogue, inspiring artists to explore hybrid forms of expression that merge organic creativity with computational innovation.

Redefining Identity in a Digital Age

As AI continues to permeate everyday life, our notions of identity are evolving. Digital identities—once a simple aggregation of profile pictures, status updates, and curated posts—are becoming complex, algorithmically mediated constructs that reflect not just who we are, but also who we might become. This evolution is driven by the ability of AI to process and analyze vast amounts of personal data, creating profiles that are far more nuanced and predictive than traditional methods ever allowed.

For example, consider the impact of AI on online communities. Platforms now use sophisticated algorithms to recommend connections, content, and even career opportunities based on an individual's digital footprint. While this can lead to highly personalized experiences, it also raises concerns about echo chambers and the narrowing of perspectives. When algorithms dictate the content we see, they can inadvertently limit our exposure to diverse ideas and challenge our ability to form independent opinions. This phenomenon has sparked debates among sociologists and digital ethicists, who warn that while AI can help forge connections, it can also reinforce divisions by amplifying existing biases.

Moreover, AI's role in shaping our digital identity extends beyond social media. In virtual and augmented reality spaces, individuals are crafting entirely new personas that blend physical and digital attributes. Avatars in virtual worlds are becoming sophisticated representations of our ideal selves, complete with customizable features and interactive behaviors that are powered by AI. These digital representations are not static—they evolve based on our interactions, preferences, and even our moods. As we navigate these virtual spaces, we are beginning to question the nature of identity itself. What does it mean to be "real" when our digital self can be as rich, dynamic, and multifaceted as our physical existence? This question lies at the heart of a broader cultural shift that is redefining the boundaries between the physical and the digital.

The Ethical Implications of AI-Driven Culture

The integration of AI into our cultural fabric brings with it a host of ethical challenges that extend beyond technical concerns. As intelligent systems influence our creative output and shape our identities, they also raise questions about autonomy, consent, and the commodification of personal data. For instance, when AI algorithms curate our social media feeds or generate art based on our online behavior, who owns the output? Who benefits from this data-driven creativity, and at what cost?

Recent research published in *Ethics and Information Technology* has examined the implications of AI in creative industries, suggesting that while these technologies offer unprecedented opportunities for innovation, they also risk undermining the human element of creativity. Critics argue that over-reliance on AI-generated content could lead to a homogenization of cultural expression, where the distinctiveness of human creativity is lost in a sea of algorithmically produced outputs. Additionally, the use of personal data to fuel creative processes raises concerns about privacy and consent, particularly when individuals are unaware of how their digital footprints are being used to generate content.

Another critical ethical issue is the potential for AI to reshape cultural narratives in ways that are subtle yet profound. As algorithms increasingly determine the content we consume, they play a significant role in shaping our worldview. A study by the MIT Media Lab found that recommendation systems on streaming platforms and news aggregators can significantly influence public opinion by curating content that reinforces existing biases. This has far-reaching implications for democracy, civic engagement, and the overall health of public discourse. In a world where AI mediates our cultural consumption, ensuring that these systems operate transparently and equitably becomes an ethical imperative.

Bridging Technology and Tradition: The Role of Human-Centric Design

Amid these sweeping changes, one thing remains clear: technology should serve to enhance, not replace, human experience. The challenge for designers, artists, and technologists is to create systems that augment our creativity while preserving the richness of human expression. This calls for a human-centric approach to AI development—one that places empathy, diversity, and inclusivity at its core.

Initiatives in value-sensitive design and participatory design are beginning to take shape, emphasizing the importance of involving a diverse range of stakeholders in the development process. By incorporating feedback from end-users, ethicists, and cultural experts, designers can create AI systems that are not only efficient but also respectful of the human context in which they operate. For example, in the field of digital art, collaborative projects that bring together artists and AI have led to innovations that retain the unpredictability and emotional depth of human creativity, even as they push the boundaries of what is technically possible.

The Interplay of Art, Media, and Technology

In today's cultural landscape, the interplay between art, media, and technology is more intricate than ever before. AI is not only a tool for creation; it is also a subject of artistic exploration. Films, novels, and digital installations are increasingly featuring AI as a central theme, exploring its impact on society, identity, and human relationships. Works like Kazuo Ishiguro's *Klara and the Sun* and Ted Chiang's short stories provoke deep reflection on the nature of intelligence, emotion, and the human condition in an age where machines can emulate human behaviors with startling accuracy.

The media, too, plays a pivotal role in shaping the public's perception of AI. Journalists and commentators are tasked with demystifying complex technologies and presenting balanced views on their potential benefits and risks. In this context, storytelling becomes a powerful medium for bridging the gap between technical innovation and everyday experience. Documentaries, podcasts, and narrative essays that examine the human side of AI provide valuable insights into how these technologies are woven into the fabric of our lives. They remind us that behind every algorithm and neural network are stories of ambition, hope, and sometimes, unintended consequences.

The Future of Digital Identity and Community

As we navigate this evolving cultural landscape, the concept of digital identity is emerging as a central theme. Our online selves are no longer confined to static profiles or isolated digital interactions; they are becoming integrated, dynamic extensions of who we are. In virtual worlds, social media platforms, and even augmented reality experiences, our identities are constantly evolving, shaped by interactions that blend the digital and the physical.

This evolution has profound implications for community and belonging. Digital platforms now enable the formation of communities that transcend geographical boundaries, allowing individuals to connect based on shared interests, values, and experiences. However, the same algorithms that facilitate these connections can also lead to echo chambers and social polarization. The challenge, then, is to design systems that promote diversity, foster genuine dialogue, and empower individuals to express their multifaceted identities. Studies by the Pew Research Center have highlighted both the potential and the pitfalls of digital communities, emphasizing the need for thoughtful design and responsible governance.

Conclusion and Transition

In this chapter, we have explored the cultural dimensions of the AI revolution—how intelligent systems are reshaping creativity, redefining our digital identities, and transforming the way we interact with art, media, and each other. From the emergence of AI as a creative collaborator to the ethical and societal challenges posed by data-driven personalization, the intersection of technology and culture is a vibrant and ever-evolving frontier.

The creative spirit that once fueled the Dot-Com Era now finds new expression in the algorithms and digital platforms that mediate our lives. As we have seen, AI is not only changing the tools we use but also the very narratives we construct about ourselves and our place in the world. Yet, as these technologies continue to advance, the need for a human-centric approach—one that values empathy, inclusivity, and transparency—becomes ever more critical.

Looking ahead, the journey into the digital future is as much about nurturing our cultural and creative identities as it is about technological innovation. In the next chapter, we will turn our focus to the practical implications of these cultural shifts—exploring how AI is influencing education, public policy, and everyday human interactions. We will examine case studies and personal narratives that illustrate the tangible impact of AI on society, and we will discuss strategies for ensuring that as technology evolves, it does so in a way that enriches our collective experience.

As we close this chapter on culture, creativity, and digital identity, we carry forward a vital insight: technology is most powerful when it serves to enhance our humanity. The story of AI is not just one of algorithms and data—it is a story about us, our aspirations, our challenges, and our shared future. With this understanding as our guide, we now step into the next phase of our exploration, where the practical realities of AI's integration into society come to the forefront. The dialogue between technology and human experience continues, inviting us to shape a future where innovation and ethical stewardship go hand in hand.

Chapter 8: Integrating the Past, Present, and Future – A Roadmap for Action

As we've journeyed through the story of artificial intelligence—from its early conceptualizations and breakthrough innovations to its transformative impact on industries, culture, and ethics—we now arrive at a critical juncture. The previous chapters have laid a comprehensive foundation: we've revisited the explosive spirit of the Dot-Com Era, traced the evolution of AI from symbolic systems to deep learning, explored today's cutting-edge innovations, envisioned tomorrow's possibilities, and grappled with the ethical and entrepreneurial challenges that accompany rapid technological change. In this final chapter, we synthesize these insights into a cohesive roadmap for action, outlining the strategies and principles needed to steer the AI revolution toward a future that is both transformative and beneficial for humanity.

Reflecting on Our Journey

The evolution of AI is not a story of isolated technological leaps, but rather a continuous, iterative process marked by periods of exuberant innovation, critical setbacks, and recalibration. The Dot-Com Era, with its heady mix of ambition and speculative risk, taught us that even the most dazzling innovations can be tempered by harsh market realities and the need for sustainable business models. Similarly, the deep learning revolution has propelled us into a new age of intelligent systems, yet it has also exposed vulnerabilities—such as algorithmic bias, opaque decision-making, and ethical quandaries—that require deliberate attention.

By reflecting on these past experiences, we can draw valuable lessons that inform our approach to the future. One key insight is that technological progress must be accompanied by thoughtful governance. History shows that unbridled innovation, without the checks and balances provided by ethical and regulatory oversight, can lead to both societal disruption and unintended consequences. As a study published in the *Harvard Business Review* reminds us, periods of rapid technological change often necessitate a parallel evolution in regulatory frameworks and cultural norms. This interplay between innovation and oversight is not a barrier to progress—it is the engine that drives sustainable, long-term transformation.

Embracing a Vision of Responsible Innovation

The future of AI depends on our ability to balance ambition with accountability. This means creating a vision of responsible innovation—one that champions not only technological excellence but also social good. Responsible innovation involves ensuring that AI systems are developed with transparency, fairness, and inclusivity at their core. It requires the active participation of diverse stakeholders, from technologists and entrepreneurs to ethicists, policymakers, and everyday citizens.

A growing body of research highlights the importance of "value-sensitive design" in this context. For example, a study in *Ethics and Information Technology* found that when developers incorporate ethical considerations from the outset, the resulting systems are more likely to align with societal values and expectations. This approach calls for a collaborative framework where technical expertise is intertwined with ethical deliberation—a model that can help preempt issues like algorithmic discrimination and privacy erosion before they become systemic problems.

The Role of Policy and Global Cooperation

No single entity or nation can tackle the multifaceted challenges posed by AI alone. The transformative power of AI is inherently global, and its impacts ripple across borders, cultures, and industries. This reality underscores the need for international cooperation and coordinated policy efforts. The European Union's proactive stance—exemplified by its General Data Protection Regulation (GDPR) and the forthcoming AI Act—serves as a model for how rigorous, forward-thinking regulation can help mitigate risks while fostering innovation.

At the same time, global initiatives like the Partnership on AI and the Global Partnership on AI are fostering dialogue among governments, corporations, and civil society. These platforms are essential for developing standards that not only protect individual rights but also promote equitable access to the benefits of AI. As recent analyses by the International Data Corporation (IDC) project global AI spending to reach astronomical levels in the coming years, the urgency of establishing a shared, ethical framework for AI development becomes ever more apparent.

Fostering an Ecosystem of Continuous Learning

Technology evolves at a breakneck pace, and nowhere is this more evident than in the realm of AI. To navigate this landscape successfully, continuous learning must become a central tenet—not only for professionals working in tech but for society as a whole. Educational institutions, corporate training programs, and public awareness campaigns all play a crucial role in preparing individuals for an AI-enabled future.

The entrepreneurial successes and failures of the Dot-Com Era illustrate the importance of adaptability and lifelong learning. In today's environment, where AI can redefine entire industries overnight, equipping the workforce with the skills to adapt is not merely an economic imperative—it is a societal one. Studies from the World Economic Forum have underscored that while AI may displace certain types of jobs, it also has the potential to create new roles that demand a blend of technical expertise and creative problem-solving. This shift calls for a reimagining of educational paradigms, with an emphasis on interdisciplinary learning that bridges technology, ethics, and the humanities.

Harnessing Innovation Through Collaboration

At the heart of this roadmap for action is the recognition that collaboration is the cornerstone of sustained innovation. The breakthroughs of the past—whether in the early internet startups or the deep learning models powering today's AI—were achieved not in isolation, but through the collective efforts of diverse teams working across disciplines. This collaborative spirit must continue as we face the challenges of tomorrow.

Collaborative innovation means building bridges between academic research and industry application, between policymakers and technologists, and between the global north and south. For example, open-source platforms like TensorFlow and PyTorch have democratized access to AI tools, enabling researchers from all corners of the globe to contribute to a shared body of knowledge. Such collaborations not only accelerate progress but also ensure that AI technologies are developed in a way that reflects a multiplicity of perspectives and experiences.

Strategies for a Future-Ready Society

As we chart the road ahead, several strategic priorities emerge for ensuring that AI serves as a force for good. First, we must institutionalize ethical oversight into every stage of AI development—from initial research to deployment. This includes adopting practices such as rigorous peer review, transparency in data and model design, and the integration of interdisciplinary ethical audits. Second, we need to invest in robust public education and workforce retraining programs that prepare individuals for the shifts in employment landscapes brought about by AI. Third, fostering an environment of global cooperation is essential. International regulatory bodies and collaborative research initiatives can help mitigate risks and create a level playing field for AI development across borders.

Furthermore, there is a need to cultivate a culture of resilience—both at the organizational and societal levels. The Dot-Com Era was marked by dramatic highs and lows, yet it ultimately paved the way for the modern digital economy by teaching us the value of learning from failure. Today, as AI continues to advance, embracing a mindset of adaptability and continuous improvement will be critical. Companies must be prepared to pivot in response to technological disruptions, and policymakers must be agile enough to adjust regulations as new challenges emerge.

The Call to Action

The future we envision is one where artificial intelligence is not an uncontrollable force but a powerful tool harnessed for the collective good. Achieving this vision requires more than just technical innovation—it demands a concerted effort from all sectors of society. Entrepreneurs, researchers, policymakers, and citizens must come together to craft a future where AI drives progress while upholding the values of equity, transparency, and respect for human dignity.

A seminal report by McKinsey & Company emphasized that the successful integration of AI into society will depend as much on human collaboration and ethical stewardship as on technological breakthroughs. This is a clarion call for us to embrace a proactive approach, one that anticipates challenges and adapts to change with foresight and compassion.

Looking Forward: The Next Steps

In this final chapter, we have integrated the lessons from the past with the innovations of today to chart a roadmap for the future. The journey from the Dot-Com Era to the present AI revolution has been one of both exhilarating progress and sobering challenges. As we stand on the threshold of tomorrow, our path forward must be guided by a commitment to responsible innovation, global cooperation, and continuous learning.

The roadmap for action outlined in this chapter is not a prescriptive formula but a framework—a set of guiding principles that can be adapted as the landscape evolves. It is a call to harness the entrepreneurial spirit of the past, the transformative power of today's technologies, and the ethical imperatives that must underpin our progress. It is a call for each of us to contribute, to stay informed, and to engage in the shaping of a future that is inclusive, innovative, and just.

As we transition to the subsequent chapters, our focus will shift to concrete examples and case studies that illustrate how these strategic principles are being applied in various sectors. We will explore the real-world implications of our roadmap—examining how AI is being leveraged to address societal challenges, create new economic opportunities, and foster a culture of innovation that respects and uplifts human values.

In the next phase of our exploration, we will delve into the interplay between technology and society, investigating how AI-driven changes are influencing everything from education and public policy to the fabric of our day-to-day interactions. We will hear from thought leaders, entrepreneurs, and everyday people whose lives are being reshaped by these transformative forces. Their stories will provide a tangible connection between the high-level strategies discussed in this chapter and the practical realities of living in an AI-driven world.

The roadmap we have charted here is a dynamic blueprint for action—one that must be continuously refined and updated in the face of rapid technological change. The road ahead is not predetermined; it is a path that we all help to forge, through innovation, dialogue, and a shared commitment to building a future that leverages AI for the common good.

Thus, as we conclude this chapter and prepare to embark on the next leg of our journey, we carry forward the insights gleaned from our exploration of ethical stewardship, global collaboration, and sustainable innovation. The future of AI is as much about our collective choices as it is about technological capabilities. With this understanding, we are ready to examine the societal dimensions of the digital transformation—exploring how AI reshapes our public institutions, influences our cultural narratives, and ultimately defines what it means to live in a connected, intelligent world.

Our journey continues, as we step into a realm where the promise of technology meets the reality of human experience—a realm where each decision, each innovation, and each collaborative effort will shape the narrative of our shared future.

Conclusion: Charting a Collective Future in the Age of AI

As we bring this journey to a close, it is essential to step back and reflect on the expansive landscape we have traversed—from the explosive spirit of the Dot-Com Era to the transformative promise of artificial intelligence. This book has sought to weave together a tapestry of insights that span historical milestones, technological breakthroughs, ethical challenges, and cultural shifts. Our exploration has revealed that AI is not simply a tool or a technological achievement; it is an ever-evolving partner in the story of human progress, one that demands a thoughtful balance between ambition and responsibility.

The Dot-Com Era, with its frenetic pace and heady mix of optimism and risk, was more than a fleeting moment of economic speculation. It was a crucible in which the modern digital world was forged. Entrepreneurs took bold leaps of faith, investors poured capital into uncharted territories, and a new culture of innovation emerged—one that celebrated failure as much as success and prized disruption over convention. That era taught us valuable lessons about the perils of unchecked exuberance and the necessity of building sustainable, resilient models in the face of rapid change. Today, as we stand on the threshold of the AI revolution, these lessons are more relevant than ever.

In retracing the evolution of artificial intelligence, we saw a rich narrative unfold—from the early philosophical inquiries of Turing and the rule-based systems of symbolic AI to the neural networks that sparked a renaissance in deep learning. The journey of AI is one of continuous refinement, marked by periods of breathtaking progress and inevitable setbacks. Each breakthrough has not only advanced our technical capabilities but has also deepened our understanding of intelligence itself. As AI systems grow more capable—learning from vast datasets, generating creative outputs, and even collaborating with humans—the challenges of scaling these innovations responsibly become increasingly apparent.

Today's AI innovations, whether in the form of generative models that create art and music or predictive systems that transform industries like healthcare and finance, stand as testaments to human ingenuity. These technologies have redefined what is possible, pushing the boundaries of creativity and efficiency. Yet, as we marvel at these achievements, we are also confronted with ethical dilemmas that require a recalibration of our values and a reimagining of our societal frameworks.

Ethical considerations are at the heart of the AI revolution. The potential for bias in AI systems, the opacity of decision-making processes, and the risks associated with deploying intelligent systems in critical domains all underscore the need for robust, transparent governance. We have learned from the past that technological progress must be tempered with accountability. The rise of explainable AI (XAI) and initiatives aimed at value-sensitive design are steps in the right direction, ensuring that as our machines become smarter, they do so in ways that are aligned with human values and ethical standards.

At the same time, the entrepreneurial ecosystem driving AI innovation is a vibrant, dynamic force that mirrors the energy of the early internet boom. Startups and venture capitalists are not only betting on new technologies—they are betting on the transformative potential of AI to redefine industries and reshape our economic landscape. However, the rush for rapid growth and disruptive innovation carries its own risks. The lessons of the Dot-Com bubble remind us that exuberance without a sustainable foundation can lead to collapse. Today's investors and entrepreneurs are increasingly aware of these challenges, seeking a balance between high-risk experimentation and the need for long-term, sustainable business models.

The interplay between technology and society is perhaps one of the most fascinating—and complex—elements of our discussion. As AI becomes more deeply integrated into our daily lives, it is redefining what it means to be human in a digital age. Our digital identities are no longer static constructs but dynamic, algorithmically mediated reflections of our behaviors, preferences, and interactions. This transformation presents both exciting opportunities and profound challenges. On one hand, personalized AI systems can enrich our lives by tailoring experiences to our unique needs. On the other hand, they can create echo chambers and reinforce existing biases, subtly shaping our perceptions and even our sense of self.

The cultural implications of AI extend far beyond our personal identities. In creative domains, AI is emerging as a collaborator—a co-creator that augments human artistic expression rather than replacing it. From visual arts to music, literature to film, AI-generated content is challenging our notions of creativity and originality. These developments invite us to consider a future where human and machine creativity are intertwined, leading to novel forms of expression that are as unpredictable as they are inspiring.

As we chart a collective roadmap for the future, several key strategies emerge. First, responsible innovation must be at the forefront of all AI development. This means integrating ethical oversight from the earliest stages of research through to deployment, ensuring that AI systems are transparent, fair, and accountable. Collaboration across disciplines is essential—not only between technologists and policymakers but also among educators, ethicists, and the broader public. By fostering an environment of continuous learning and dialogue, we can better navigate the uncertainties of rapid technological change.

Second, global cooperation is indispensable. The challenges posed by AI are not confined by national borders; they are global in scope. International regulatory frameworks and collaborative research initiatives are critical for ensuring that the benefits of AI are equitably distributed and that the risks are effectively managed. Recent regulatory efforts, such as the European Union's GDPR and the emerging AI Act, highlight the need for proactive, harmonized policies that can keep pace with the speed of innovation. At the same time, public and private sectors must work together to develop best practices and standards that promote ethical AI development on a global scale.

Third, we must invest in the future of work and education. As AI reshapes the economic landscape, it is imperative that we prepare our workforce for the changes ahead. This involves rethinking traditional educational models, promoting lifelong learning, and creating robust retraining programs that help individuals transition to new roles. The evolution of work in the AI era is not a zero-sum game; it is an opportunity to create jobs that are more aligned with human strengths—jobs that require creativity, empathy, and complex problem-solving skills. By investing in human capital, we ensure that technological progress translates into widespread societal benefit.

Finally, we must embrace a mindset of resilience and adaptability. The journey from the Dot-Com Era to the present AI revolution has been punctuated by cycles of rapid innovation and necessary recalibration. This dynamic process is likely to continue as we confront new challenges and opportunities. Embracing failure as a learning opportunity, maintaining flexibility in our strategies, and continually reassessing our goals are essential components of a future-ready society. The entrepreneurial spirit that drove the early days of the internet is not only a historical artifact but a living, evolving force that can guide us through the uncertainties of tomorrow.

In conclusion, the roadmap we have charted throughout this book is a call to action—a call for a collective, interdisciplinary effort to harness the transformative power of AI while safeguarding the values that define our humanity. We have seen how the lessons of the past, the innovations of the present, and the ethical imperatives of the future converge to create a vision for responsible progress. The journey from the explosive beginnings of the Dot-Com Era to the current AI revolution is a testament to human ingenuity, resilience, and the unyielding pursuit of progress.

As we close this exploration, we must recognize that the future of AI is not predetermined. It is a path we forge together through informed decision-making, thoughtful regulation, and a commitment to inclusive innovation. Every stakeholder—be it an entrepreneur, a policymaker, a researcher, or an everyday citizen—has a role to play in shaping this future. By integrating the insights gained from our historical reflections, technological assessments, and ethical deliberations, we can build a future where AI serves as a catalyst for positive change, enhancing our collective well-being and empowering us to tackle the grand challenges of our time.

The discussion does not end here. Rather, it sets the stage for a new chapter—a phase of active engagement where theory meets practice, and where the vision of a technologically advanced yet ethically grounded society begins to take shape. Our journey has illuminated the vast potential of AI and the profound responsibilities it entails. The road ahead is filled with promise, but it demands vigilance, collaboration, and an unwavering commitment to the principles that underpin a just and equitable society.

As we transition from this conclusion, we invite you to join us in the next phase of our exploration—an in-depth look at the practical integration of AI into our daily lives. In the forthcoming discussions, we will delve into specific case studies and personal narratives that exemplify how these technologies are not only reshaping industries but also redefining our cultural and social landscapes. The interplay between technology and humanity will continue to be the central theme of our collective story, a story that we are writing together, one innovation at a time.

The future is not a distant destination—it is here, unfolding in real time. With the lessons of the past as our compass and a shared vision for a better tomorrow as our guide, we stand ready to embrace the next chapter of our technological journey. Let us move forward with determination, wisdom, and the courage to shape a future where technology amplifies the best of what it means to be human.